DOMINIC HOLLAND

TAKES on life

VOL.1

To Ana

One per day and no
More !

[signature]

To the

we you day are in

think!

Acknowledgements

A happy nod to my good friend Marcus Landau of Conker Design for creating yet another funky cover.

My thanks to Morna Walters of Puzzle-Communications. Rishi Sunak had nothing for me in Lockdown but Morna came through by putting me on to Patreon and the flurry of content that this required spawned the idea for this book.

I am grateful to my band of loyal Patrons for their encouragement and support. Fortunately, and thank goodness, they are too numerous to mention by name but they know who they are.

And finally, my thanks to the people who have inspired the majority of these *Takes*; my four boys but especially my wife, Nikki. All those years ago, when she said 'I do', unwittingly she became an early reader of many millions of my words and counting. What follows are my good words. My best writing, so you can imagine then, the drivel that Nikki has needed to get through.

If this book is a success, no one will be more deserving than Nikki Holland - or as relieved.

Introduction

I write this introduction with some caution because this book is intended to be funny; to make my readers actually laugh. Not on every page nor in every *take;* some are intended to be thoughtful and even dare-I-say-it, poignant. And I don't mean laugh in the way that my audiences laugh when I am doing my proper job being a stand-up comedian. But because I can make people laugh on-stage, does this mean I can do the same from the page? You can be the judge of this.

I am dubious of many books described as funny and sometimes even hilarious. Too often this is mis-selling. Wry at best. Or even worse, wistful.

As a stand-up, there is not much money in wry or wistful. Even chuckles are not so lucrative. Audible laughs are what we feed on and I write this book with the same intentions.

That said, I am not a writer. Not really. I'm more of a dabbler, albeit an experienced one. This is best explained by Iron Man in the Spider-Man movie *Far From Home*. Iron Man is encouraging a young Peter Parker to join The Avengers and he wants to make this announcement to the world's press who have gathered at his behest.

"Peter, through these doors are the world's press. Proper writers. **No bloggers...***"*

This made me roar with laughter because I am a blogger and so not a proper writer. I have written for newspapers. I've had columns in nationals. My own and ones I've ghosted. I've written novels, screenplays, radio series and the odd sit-com. But mostly nowadays, I am a blogger and it is my blog that is the spine of this book.

The kid in the aforementioned movie is my son btw. Peter Parker. Not the character but the actor. Tom Holland is my eldest son and the reason I started my blog in 2010 which I called *Eclipsed*. If you don't understand this blog title, then it is unlikely you will enjoy this book.

What follows here is not an explanation of how this familial peculiarity came to pass; that my son should eclipse me in show-biz and whilst still a teenager. I have written and published that painful story already. Time to move on, I feel.

This book is a force for good; a reproduction of some of my favourite blogs but mostly new anecdotes and imponderables written especially for this tome.

Expect some wisdom. Some sage advice and much humility from a quirky little man who stoically copes with numerous life struggles. And this somewhat blighted life, coupled with an ability to make people laugh out loud bodes well for a book that intends to enliven reader's spirits and make people feel good about themselves.

A self-help book then, but one without the worthiness. And one that actually helps, I hope.

There follows thirty-one essays *(Takes)* and this number is deliberate. Because I expect that this book will occupy many toilets, I provide a *Take* for each day and to last for even the longest month. Therefore, if it takes you longer than a month to read, then you will know that you are not emptying your bowel frequently enough to be healthy. An immediate upside and like I said, a book that is good for you.

Thirty-one takes. Some short, some longer but none long enough for the truly bunged up. Some funny and some thoughtful.

Vignettes of life is how they might be described but this is too pretentious for my tastes. The same with musings-on-life and yet...

Takes feels about right to me. My take/s on your life and mine.

Thank you for coming along. I trust you are sitting comfortably and I hope you enjoy it.

Take One

Mightier than the Sword…

The English language is a very powerful thing. Something that our small country has and everyone else wants. The world language and the first language of the human being.

Based on only twenty-six letters and yet we have the plays of Shakespeare, the novels of Dickens and the songs by The Beatles.

Our language is empowering but it can also be terrifying. Simple words that can strike us dumb with fear.

Replacement bus service…

To set out on a train journey and find oneself waiting for a bus seems to me to be an utter betrayal and made worse by the temerity of calling this a 'service.'

Health and Safety…

Whilst we cherish our health and we all want to feel safe – when these two words are combined, most rational people will flinch.

Health and Safety Officer…

An Officer and a Gentleman is a movie starring a handsome young Richard Gere. He plays an officer in the US navy who, adorned in his smart white officers uniform, sweeps Deborah Winger off her feet. The film works and was a box office smash. Safe to say that this film would not have worked had Gere played a Health and Safety officer and tried to carry a woman out of a factory wearing his high vis vest. Impossible anyway, because to lift a woman up requires a back brace at the very least…

Welcome to Ringo.

A phone-call to the parking app we all make with trepidation as the men on mopeds circulate like jackals waiting for an elderly person whose phone is in need of a software update.

But the words that terrorise us above all others are;

You are running low on magenta…

Or it might be Cyan that your printer is complaining about being short of. Which is infuriating because you can't recall printing anything in Cyan. Ever. Cyan is blue by the way. But Cyan to some nerd at Hewlett Packard who wants to big up his role in life. Same with magenta which is purple to you and me. Prince was widely regarded as a musical maestro, even a genius and certainly a man of extravagant flamboyance and yet not even he dared to sing Magenta Rain.

And finally, some words that we hear but will always ring hollow.

Words said but are intended to be ignored. Recited only to comply with regulations.

Please gamble responsibly.

Words that come at the end of an advert for a Bingo website or a bookmaker. Typically, adverts with jolly music featuring happy people having enormous fun. The overall feeling is that of a club. And you can join too. Here's a welcoming free bet.

Many people do gamble within the limits of what they can afford. But many do not. And a great many will gamble away their entire livelihoods. Lose their home, marriages and even their lives.

Not that any bookmaker wants their patrons to lose their shirts and take their own lives.

But equally, they don't want winners either. Or not too many anyway. Winners on betting sites will have their accounts curtailed with bet limits placed.

What bookmakers really want are losers.

And really, how *responsible* is this?

Take Two

Best Laid Plans?

Many moons ago I was invited to play in a celebrity golf day at the prestigious London Club in Kent. I was moderately famous at the time but still I felt a little self-conscious meeting my fellow players and registering their disappointment. To be fair, I did rank middle to low on the table of available celebrities. A league headed by Hugh Grant no less and then came Ronnie Corbett plus an array of sports stars from the world of rugby and football. Usually there are not enough celebrities to go around but, on this day, there was a surfeit and so my four-ball contained two 'celebrities' and two paying punters.

Myself (comedian, author but these days, mainly blogger) and Jonathan Whalley, the actor. I know, me neither. But I am delighted to be paired with Jonathan (known as Johnny, albeit still not better known). Instantly, we form an obscurity bond and we can share our playing partners' celebrity disappointment.

I arrive at the course in good time and park my turquoise Fiat Multipla (3 seats in the front!) amongst the mainly German cars, mostly two seaters and with excessively large exhaust pipes. With me are my golf clubs, what I am wearing, a waterproof jacket (just on the-off-chance) and nothing else. No umbrella. No change of clothes for the inevitable dinner/prize giving. Not a jacket, let alone a shirt and tie. But I am fighting fit and just like Prince Andrew, I hardly sweat and so my golf attire will be pristine and suitable for the meal.

And it's June, so what chance of rain?

Let's play golf.

By the ninth hole, the rain is coming in harder than golf balls. Almost horizontal. The temperature has plummeted. Johnny and I are both soaked to the bone and freezing cold. My waterproof jacket is as hapless as the suede shoe protector that we always fall for. It is not possible for me to be anymore wet. Johnny is older than me and visibly suffering. I notice that his fingers have turned blue and I start to panic that he is about to have a heart attack or this being a golf course, his final ever stroke.

Suddenly, off in the distance a hooter sounds.

The golf is abandoned for unplayable conditions and not before time.

I drive the buggy home fast. Foot to the floor but Johnny is a heavy man and we are both sodden. I need to get him warm and dry and I wonder if there is a doctor amongst our party.

The club house is mobbed with wet and freezing golfers. Into the dressing rooms, Johnny jumps in a hot shower to revive and only then my predicament dawns on me.

All around me, men are stripping off their wet clothes. Next to them are suit bags with jackets and ironed shirts. Holdalls containing clean underwear and socks. Some even have toiletry bags. One guy is shaving. Another is blow drying his hair.

Johnny is towelling down already and is clearly not going to die. I have saved his life and now it is me who needs rescuing.

What the hell am I going to do?

In the shower I am no more wet than I was on the course but at least I am warm. But for my cold thoughts; the only things waiting for me are my soaking wet clothes.

The only sensible thing to do is to make my apologies and just leave. Obviously, I can't attend the dinner. What was I thinking? Sorry, I had a brain freeze and have arrived completely unprepared. But it is rude not to attend the dinner and the fund-raising auction. It is the reason why these days are organised.

Men are dried and dressed now. Warm and comfortable. Meanwhile I have a plan; to blow dry my clothes but I worry if I can do this without drawing unusual looks.

Instead I decide to iron my clothes dry. Brilliant. Wrapped in a towel, I find an employee and request an ironing board. It arrives and I begin, ignoring any incredulous looks as I start to iron a sock. If anyone asks, I will explain that I just have very high standards. I set the iron to linen and put my steaming sock aside and move on to my more important collared tee-shirt.

I decide that my underpants and socks are done for.

No-socks is a look now. But back then it certainly wasn't, so what must people have thought of me and yet this would be the least of my problems.

I pull on my still wet tee shirt and then my damp trousers. And with as much dignity as I can muster, I make my way in to the bar and the throng. Wet clothes and no socks. The classic sports casual look, completed with my chin held high.

Immediately I am aware of unusual looks. But what are people staring at? Not at my celebrity. Not when Hugh Grant is in the room.

One guy approaches me.

"What is that on your chest?"

I look down but I can't see anything untoward. I brush the fabric and it feels different.

Back in the locker room I stare in a mirror with horror. On my chest is a burn stain in the perfect shape of an iron. I have three options. To pretend it's a design thing by burning the other side of the tee-shirt in exactly the same way. To dispense with 'sports casual' and dine topless.

Or to burst in to tears.

But then Johnny Whalley steps up to rescue me. Johnny has a spare shirt which he is happy to lend me.

This is good news but with some very obvious downsides. Johnny is a big man. It is not so rude to suggest that he has grown in to his surname. Six feet tall and at least sixteen stone. His white shirt drowns me. It's more cassock than shirt and I look like an altar boy, the absence of socks adding to my celestial look.

Ronnie Corbett would have been a better match up but I would never have asked one of my comedy heroes if he had a spare outfit.

Back in the bar, it is busy. Packed with ruddy-faced men determined to add to their colour. By some distance, I am the least comfortable person in the bar. I suspect that I am the only man who is commando. And my voluminous shirt looks like I am suffering with a horrendous wasting disease. The London club is an American style golf club. A large open plan clubhouse with lots of different levels and all interconnected with small flights of stairs. Not ideal then for a man with his ankles on show.

And now for an admission to add to this debacle...

I was quite excited at the prospect of meeting Hugh Grant. You see, at this time of my life I had two films (screenplays) at varying stages of not being made, although I didn't know this at the time. And the prospect of meeting and getting to know a genuine movie star was very tempting.

Who you know and all that...

But during one of my frequent visits to the locker room throughout the meal, I decided that introducing myself to Mr Grant in such circumstances would be counter-productive.

I duly bought my raffle tickets but I didn't wait for the draw. Knowing my luck, I would break a habit of a lifetime and my numbers would be drawn. And I would have to walk to the front of the room to collect my prize. A new top perhaps and some socks? At the earliest possible opportunity and without being rude, I headed home leaving behind my underpants, socks and my tee-shirt.

I laundered Johnny's shirt and duly sent it to him with a letter of thanks.

I never did meet Mr Grant and I never did get those films made. But even though, since then I have endured many rounds of abject golf, I have never felt so vanquished and humiliated by the game as I did on this day and yet somehow it remains a game that I love.

Take Three

The Lion King

Safaris are something to tick off, wouldn't you agree?

And just to say that I am self-aware enough to realise just how 'first world' and privileged this sounds, but I needn't apologise because it happens to be true.

In Kenya then with my family over Christmas, we are out on the plains every day in an open top Land Cruiser. I am about to sound even more cosseted and 'first world' now because this vehicle doesn't exactly cruise. Cruising implies ease and luxury which is not easily accomplished on the African plains. In Africa, it is impossible to cruise even on the roads. The land is dry, dusty and cracked. It is hard work and particularly punishing on the vehicles. Attritional on the occupants too and especially if like me, you are prone to car sickness.

And all to be endured in order to see a lion. Basically.

There are other animals available. Rhinos and Leopards are highly prized but we are told that these are so rare and remote that they can only ever be glimpsed.

But lions are present and we are excited to see Simba and the family.

As well as herds of other animals. Thousands of herbivores like zebra and gazelles and whilst they are majestic, they are so plentiful that they quickly wane. Bait for the lions is how I come to see them and I hope that one of them might do the right thing and volunteer as a straggler and wake the lions from their stupor.

Back at our camp, we meet other families and from all over the world.

One lady is leaving tomorrow to go home to Texas and is unhappy because she had come to see Tigers.

In Africa!

I don't say anything but I do ponder...

America - the world's First country and yet so unique. The country that gave us The Lion king and more recently, The Tiger King...

And with this, a phrase comes to my mind and it makes me smile... *Only in America*, the title of my first novel.

Back on the plains for the Hollands. The intrepid six. In search of Simba but not Tigger.

The guides always stop their trucks to converse with each other. I expect they share information on which animals are where and ideally, where the f*** is Simba.

While the two driver's chat is usually an awkward wait for the two waiting parties. Two well-to-do families briefly acknowledging each other with a smile and perhaps a little wave.

But on one such occasion, something remarkable happened.

The family in the other Cruiser – mum, dad and two daughters are staring at us. The girls are staring at Tom and the dad is staring at me.

The aridity, the sun glare, the dust and the sun cream plays havoc with how we look and it is not so easy to recognise even familiar faces. But there is something about this bloke and he is definitely staring at me. And I wonder…

"Dominic… Is that you?" He calls out and his Welsh accent confirms it.

This is the Davis family.

Jonathan Davis is one of the world's greatest rugby players of his generation. In both codes of the game (union and league) and in Europe and Australia, he played at the very highest level. And for Wales of course, where rugby is the official religion.

A man I have done many dinners with over the years and who I greatly admire. Not much bigger than me, to have the bravery to dominate a sport like rugby is remarkable leaving aside his audacious skill and guile.

We catch up briefly. Both stunned that we should meet in the middle of the Masai Mara, Kenya. Ordinarily we would hop out and properly catch up but it's a little dangerous I guess with Simba and family in residence (apparently). Plus, I am sure that his daughters would like to meet me also (and probably Tom as well).

As our vehicles part, I am stoked at the encounter. As excited as I would be at seeing any animal. I explain to Tom about Jonathan's illustrious rugby career. How he played for Wales…

And with this, Tom came out with a killer line.

You see every four years, the best rugby players from the British Isles tour either Australia, South Africa or New Zealand on a rotating basis. Outside the World Cup, it is the biggest event in the rugby calendar. And the British team is called The British Lions.

"Blimey dad. We've come all the way to Kenya to see the lions and we end up seeing a British Lion."

Take Four

Too Cool for School

Clothes are a way for me to keep warm and to preserve my modesty.

But for many people, clothes are much more than this.

I like clothes. I can admire them but I don't do them. Not really. I have neither the money nor the inclination to buy the latest clobber nor the energy to keep up. And I am slightly resentful or suspicious of people who do.

Also, I am sceptical of the fashion world in general, its ethics and its earnest over-reach. There is an air of bullying to fashion, I think. That woman from Vogue who famously never smiles and wears sunglasses indoors. And the over-use of the word 'genius'. Our world is blessed with people of genius and thank goodness. In my view, the surgeon who pioneered removing a healthy heart from a dead person and plonking it in to another person is unquestionably a contender for genius. But much less so, the person who dreamt up the mini-skirt. It's just a skirt but shorter FFS.

In my life I have found myself in many situations where I do not belong. And even more so since my son has become famous and in high demand. But Tom Holland is rarely available whereas I on the other hand...

One such occasion was a private dinner in a tent in London. It came my way via Tom's private bankers. As I recall they were the sponsors of this dinner-in-a-tent and naturally they wanted to fill the place with their illustrious clients. But high net worth clients with their hectic schedules and general apathy, the bank started to panic and even started reaching out to parents.

Typically, of me, I had not really taken on board what I was agreeing to attend in Tom's absence. Just that it is nice to be asked and it is rude to say no. So along I went on the train into London.

The tent is not a tent at all but a beautiful marquis and is temporarily located in the middle of Barclay Square in Mayfair.

And to raise money for no doubt a very worthy charity, so dutifully I stop at a cash-point en-route because there is bound to be a raffle.

As soon as I arrive I feel conspicuous. The marquis is beautiful with all the mod cons. Heating. Sprung floors, fully carpeted, luxurious toilets, a free bar and two floors.

Security is tight, obviously. Wealthy people are in attendance and in some instances, their much less well-off parents. On the ground floor is an art and antique exhibition with the dinner to be held upstairs. I spot famous people immediately. Actors and minor Royals. Gary Lineker is the only person who I know but he is ensconced in conversation so I don't bother him. I decide to peruse the art instead, in case there is anything that takes my fancy before dinner.

Upstairs is high chic. Three enormous refectory tables are laid out for dinner. Opulent and decadent. It looks like a set from that unwatchable movie, Eyes Wide Shut. Which we only sat through for one reason and one reason only and was therefore a bitter disappointment.

The table settings are a work of art. The place is all dry ice, ice sculptures and with extravagant ornaments clinging to the walls and ceiling. Nudes adorn the walls, naturally. By now, I have learned that a very famous chef is busy preparing dinner for us all. I suspect that many people attending would call it supper.

The whole place is achingly cool and I am delighted to be attending a dinner that I am not required to speak at. But still my instincts kick in and I start to probe for lines and an opening to a stand-up set in such a room.

I learn that the whole evening is inspired by and a homage to the late great fashion designer, Alexander McQueen. Everything before us is McQueen. Even the plates are his design and I am suitably intimidated. The charity receiving our support this evening is also McQueen's. To raise money for people struggling to gain a foothold in the fashion industry.

A tough sell then for the auctioneer.

'Ladies and gentlemen, your kind donations tonight will help to support the visionary designers of tomorrow. The people who make clothes that hardly anyone will ever wear…'

Usually at such events, I am all-in for supporting and chipping in. Brain-injured children or Diabetes, (type 1 I mean and not type 2 fatties, obviously) but helping to create the next Vivienne Westwood?

I take my seat and introduce myself to my fellow diners. To

my left is a man dressed in an outfit that tells me he did not take the train into town. His clobber is like the TK Max Gold Label rail that not even the maximum discounts can shift. He is something to do with Elton John, his manager perhaps and this makes good sense. To my right is the place setting for Nikki Holland who is absent because she is unwell. Directly opposite me is a bloke; an ordinary Joe who like me, must have been a last-minute call up. Immediately we bond and become friends.

Nikki's absence is my fault. Had I bothered to read the particulars of the evening then I would know that this was not just a dinner. But a formal dining experience. Attendees are accounted for and place settings laid. In my in-box will be a series of emails (in bold) asking me to confirm the attendance of both parents of the actor, Tom Holland. As such there is only one spare seat in the entire room and it is next to me.

You may know at the Oscars Ceremony that an army of plebs are used to fill seats in the stalls as celebs go to the loo to relieve themselves. Or, as likely, to powder their nose in order to get through the ceremony.

Well this happened here. The dinner organiser; someone I imagine to be like Fronk from the Steve Martin movie, Father of the Bride, spotted the vacant seat and with eyes agog, clapped his delicate hands above one of his ears and a lady from his team was dispatched to fill Nikki's chair.

She sat down quietly and barely introduced herself. She had that cultivated tortured look. Sullen and bleak. There was little chance of any smiles. Laughter is usually a great ice breaker and I like a challenge but I know my funny limits. My new friend opposite and I understood that we had our work cut out and that our debate about which Charlie's Angel we most fancied growing up was definitely over.

She worked for Alexander McQueen and it appeared that this was the only ground and subject on which she was prepared to engage. His genius. His vision. His creativity. The evening was created in his eye…

To all of this I nodded sagely but without being able to contribute very much.

Our meals arrived – a stunning array of beef already carved and served on central sharing platters. Our compliments to the chef and our thanks also because I had been expecting nut roast, tofu and tree bark. Which did arrive for our new dining companion who was aghast to be so close to so much bloody meat and yet this was still marginally less offensive than us.

She confused me by referring to the great man as 'Lee' and my questioning this was met by a heavy sigh that I didn't know Lee was his Christian name and how he was known to his friends. I half apologised but I didn't bother to explain that my only knowledge of Lee was his success, his troubles and his very sad suicide.

Which is a good way to tee up what was to come. Not dessert but the best faux pas I have ever witnessed.

As is so often with stilted conversations, a willing participant starts to reach, clutch and flounder and this was me. My friend opposite though, had given up completely. But then he suddenly snapped to, as though I had kicked him awake and he had a question of his own.

'Is he coming tonight?'

She looked at him with a quizzical look, as did I. Hers though was a look of confusion. Wondering if she had heard him correctly. I knew that she had. But she needed clarification and my man was right on point.

'This Lee or Alexander or whatever his name is. Is he here tonight?'

Her shoulders slumped. Her face, a study in sadness. But not for poor old Lee but for the ignorant clown opposite her.

'You must be the only person here who doesn't know that Lee is dead.'

To be fair to my new friend, his reaction to this withering question was superb. He could have crumpled and begged for forgiveness. Or ridiculously offered his condolences. But not this guy. No, no. This hero doubled down.

'Well… that'll be a no then.'

The dessert was superb but she did not stick around to enjoy it and we got back to where we'd left off.

And quickly, we agreed.

Hands down, Farah Fawcett Majors.

Take Five

At your Service...

We live in hierarchies and we all know where we stand, right?

Tallest? Best looking? Wealthiest? Funniest? Most successful...

What we do for a living, from the vaunted professions down... we are all workers. Workers with our names on our shirts, our desks, the office door or finally on the building itself.

The road is a good metaphor for hierarchy and specifically the motorway or the highway.

Because what car you drive is so much more than just a mode of travelling.

Your ride is a statement.

A muscle car with an excessive and overly aggressive exhaust. Anyone?

No, me neither.

Or what about a vintage car as a marker down, with its trade-off between great looks but not starting.

Or the convertible car - for people who don't like chatting but do like flies.

The sports car of course. The gleaming Ferrari or the dark and menacing Porsche. Although here in the UK with speed cameras as prevalent as speed humps, I can only imagine the frustration at paying extra for speed that is impossible to use.

And then the veritable daddy of them all; the Rolls Royce. The ultimate status symbol on the road.

Rich, important person coming through. Get the f*** out of my way.

A house is a great indicator of status. And speaking of hierarchies, with our Prince Harry becoming plain old Harry Wales and moving to LA, the media have revelled in explaining the value of Tyler Perry's house that was their stop gap before they found a cake of their own.

But a house is static. It can't be seen and shown off when we are out and about - unless we take a realtors brochure with us to show people.

And so then, the car is a mobile demonstration of wealth and status. And as such the Rolls Royce Phantom ($400,000) is sort of like a mobile home? Albeit neither Mr Rolls nor Mr Royce would thank me for this association – but you know what I mean?

And there is a hierarchy on the road also...

The fast lane for the fast people. The people who are frenetic and go-get. And presumably for those who are also just late.

The middle lane for the plodders. The Steady Eddies who will arrive safely and in-time but so what - because they're never gonna light up any room.

And then the slow lane of course, for the elderly and the petrified. The drivers who are not restricted by any speed limits. 70 miles per hour is an option but not a possibility.

All of these things... what we drive and how we drive are signals of who we are – which is why I so enjoy the motorway service station, because suddenly we are all the same.

At the services, we are all just motorists who need a break. To stretch our legs. To possibly fill one tank and almost certainly to empty another. Men of a certain age might even take the opportunity to do the emptying twice. As they arrive and before they leave. One for the road, so to speak.

And unlike airports, the motorway service station is hierarchy free.

There is no first-class lounge.

In a service station, we all muck in together. A melting pot of humanity. Cheek by jowl (pre and post covid, obviously) the great unwashed next to the highly preened and sanitised.

In the service station and on foot, the status imbued by our car is gone.

Mr Rolls without his ride is now just an ordinary Joe like you and I, although he might still be identifiable. He might have nicer shoes. An expensive watch perhaps but he doesn't get a special place to pee. He uses the exact same toilet facilities as the rest of us. No heated seat or attendant to shake anything here. And in my experience, it is best not to stare too closely at someone in a public lavatory and especially not at a man's watch.

There are other giveaways of Mr Rolls. He is less likely to join the snaking queue for KFC or McDonalds.

In the UK, we have large warning signs aligning our roads – TIREDNESS KILLS. TAKE A BREAK.

But in the longer term, so can fast food laden with saturated fat but I keep this to myself as I pick my sandwich and wait for my coffee.

A coffee smug, perhaps?

And this is why I enjoy the motorway service station. For its sense of representation and being such a leveller. Where we are all the same no matter who we are or what our means.

And then back on the road again, in my sensible car and in the slow or middle lane, I know that the Ferrari I spotted parked up at the services will soon come flashing by me, a blur of throbbing red in the fast lane and screaming for everyone's attention. And I too, duly pay homage. Because for sure, this is a car of great beauty and something to behold. And who can detract from the magnificent engineering and history of such a marque.

But ahead is a speed camera you Bell-End and I hope you get pinged.

And with this - Snap - we are back in the hierarchy again.

And life goes on…

Take Six

Survival is King

As a parent I have much to be grateful for and for many reasons, some more obvious than others. Just having healthy kids is a blessing and one that we all take for granted until we see a parent with a child who will never fly the nest. But problems are relative and most mums and dads just muddle on through with fervent hopes and fingers crossed.

As a dad, naturally I have hoped that my kids might be good at things. That said, one of the things I am most grateful for, is that all of my boys were shit at swimming.

In my family, swimming has been important but only for the purposes of remaining alive. As in, to not drown.

But I am aware that there is much more to swimming than merely, not drowning. Medals and Cups. Even Olympic gongs for the hallowed few. But this is of no interest to anyone in the Holland household, thank you very much.

And why?

Because, surely its every parent's nightmare being told by a swimming coach that their kid has talent.

'They might even be good enough for the swim team.'

There are more harrowing words that a parent can hear, but not many.

"We swim four times a week from 5.30 a.m."

This utterly hideous scenario poses a moral conundrum for any normal parent…

Is it ever acceptable to weigh down a child before they try out for the swim team?

The Holland boys can all swim. But not well. Basic front crawl (head out of the water stuff, mostly). Rudimentary breast stroke possibly, but certainly no butterfly. No one in the history of being compromised in water has ever butterflied to safety.

I have known many parents caught in the competitive swimming trap. They are easy to spot with their Panda eyes and dogged insistence that swimming is a great sport.

No, it isn't. Not really.

Where is the fun?

I don't mean in swimming. Where is the fun in swimming? Of course, swimming is enormous fun, as in frolicking about. Indeed, swimming is the mainstay of the family holiday. Splashing, dunking, spurting, hand-stands, hand flips, chatting, flirting, petting and let's be honest, on occasion, even full-blown shagging. All hugely popular leisure activities, enjoyed the world over and in every language.

But competitive swimming?

Leaving aside the actual race and even winning, just consider the work that is required in order to get on to those blocks.

Lengths and lengths of the pool. Nothing but lengths. Over and over. Back and forth. And all for some Nazi in a tracksuit with a whistle, a stop watch and a scowl.

At least on a run or a cycle, people can interact with one another, although I think joggers who like to chat should probably up their game. But try chatting with the chap in the next swimming lane and you're likely to drown.

And what future for the great school swimmer?

I recall many times when I have played tennis on holiday and rued not learning to play the game properly. No tennis court is long enough for my forehand. No net is low enough for my backhand. But I have never been on holiday and wished I could smash out a 50m freestyle.

On holiday, I have met other families and 'friendly' tennis matches have been arranged but never a swimming race. No dad has ever challenged me to a couple of lengths of the pool. And if one did, then I would run a mile and swim nowhere.

No doubt, there are health gains to swimming but no more so than other more sociable activities, like walking.

An indisputable swimming gain, however, is the swimmers physique; often held up as the pinnacle of human physicality. We've all ogled the swimmers in the Olympics.

When they line up on their blocks, I am awestruck. By their talent. Their fortitude. Their sacrifice. Their dedication. Their majesty. But mostly because they are all so darn fit. Human dolphins with figures to match. And yet my interest wanes the moment they hit the water.

And finally, can we spare a moment for the long-distance swimmers. These lions of the sea. How tough it is on these poor wretch's because they don't acquire God-like physiques for their efforts. They make the effort to abandon the clean and warm swimming pool for the ocean with its detritus of condoms and nappies and commit to swimming not lengths but blinking miles. Miles and miles. And yet for all this effort they are not rewarded with the sleek physique. They are in fact, more whale-like than dolphin and this seems to me to be a particularly cruel equation.

Many millions of years ago, we emerged from the sea. And with good reason. Why go back?

There is no need.

Take Seven

Attempted Conversations with my Agent…

Agents are one of the new 'professions' that are largely unnecessary. Individuals positing themselves between a transaction of buyer and seller – oiling a 'need' and a 'have' and doing very nicely in the process thank you very much. What I mean is, if agents ceased to exist, these transactions would continue on regardless.

Like being a critic, no one sets out to be an agent. Not really.

But I am afraid that agents have arrived and they are not going anywhere. And particularly so in my world of show-business, darling.

In entertainment, an agent is essential. Even a hapless one.

Over my stop start career, I have had numerous agents charged with making me money. The great and the good. All of them useless and no doubt they would all say the same about me.

Stand-Up comedy is often cited as the hardest job of all. The stresses and strains of seeking laughs and the enormous odds against becoming famous and extravagantly well paid.

Some years ago, sitting at a service station on my way to a gig that pays the same buttons as it did decades ago and feeling disconsolate, I thought to call my agent.

Not my comedy agent but my commercial agent.

Bear with me.

A commercial agent is an expert at placing 'talent' in commercials; voice overs and on-screen ads which can be highly lucrative and nice work if one can get it.

Which in the main, I can't.

But I did once procure the services of a highly reputable commercial agent. He had seen my show in Edinburgh and with my quick wit, my quirky face and his contacts, we decided that we could make hay together.

Sitting in my car I scrolled down my phone for his number. It had been a long time since we had spoken. Too long and so it would be good to catch up. To see how he is (and what the fuck he's been doing...)

The agency name bore his surname but the telephonist paused when I asked to speak with him. Being highly emotionally intelligent, immediately my antennae twitched. Something was wrong. Had I been let go from their books? Culled from the agency in one of their annual reviews.

No.

It was worse than this.

But what then? Has he left the agency? That would be odd, since this is his agency.

The lady on the phone explained that he was dead.

Immediately I floundered. Oh lord, how terrible, the poor man. Aren't comedians supposed to be quick on their feet and have good timing?

The poor man. So many questions I wanted to ask. When, how, why? He wasn't old. I think he was married. His poor children. His wife. The shock. And when is the funeral?

I should send flowers. And should I go to the funeral? Yes, that would be nice. To pay my respects. If I can make it, that is. If I have the spare time? Which I do. It's because I have so much spare time that I am calling.

When, is the question that I settle on. Not the funeral but when did my poor friend and colleague die?

This is what I ask and it is greeted by another aching pause. A vacuum for me to flail in.

"Two years ago."

I am instantly winded.

Fuck me. Two years ago.

My agent had died two years ago and I didn't even know.

And shameful to admit but instantly my sympathy shifts - and in classic show-biz narcissism style, back to me.

Because what does this say about my career? Presumably the

agency informed certain clients of his tragic death. The clients who were successful and being cast in commercials. And surely, they would also have appointed a new agent to continue representing this 'talent.'

I didn't ask the poor receptionist if I might be put through to this new agent. Too insensitive all-round. The writing was on the wall and written large.

And then another instinct of mine immediately kicks in; namely my delusional optimism.

I assure myself that I remain a successful comedian. I am busy. Just an hour down the road, a room full of people are waiting for me to make them all laugh for twenty minutes. And for £200 cash.

I pick up my coffee which I note is half full and not half empty. This is good news and typical of me. I pull on my seat belt and start my car. And speaking of clutching, I remind myself that things aren't so bad. I am still alive to start with which in this context...

Take Eight

M'Lud

Let me set the scene; somehow, I am involved in a golf match at a club that I am not eligible to join and wouldn't wish to even if I could afford the fees. An old school type of golf club. The members have Aga's, black Labradors and red trousers to match their faces. They are often unfeasibly tall and this means they literally look down on people.

My opponent is a better golfer than me and we quickly establish that he is better than me at everything. A judge no less, he is older, wiser, taller, richer, cleverer…

This being his home club, it is his honour to hit off first and rather fittingly, his honour kept the honour throughout our entire match.

At the turn, I am three down. I am feeling miserable and not just because of my golf. But because of him. Naturally I am inquisitive and genuinely interested in people. At the half way stage of our match, I have established the following; that he had been at boarding school and Oxford, that he has two children, both of whom had also been at Oxford, that he has a London city flat, a spread in Cheltenham and a gaff in the Caribbean.

Nice. And he knows nothing about me at all apart from the obvious. That I can't putt and should never be conceded anything (I get nervous).

He did know I was a comedian but only by my introduction; I hadn't made his eminence even smile thus far.

He goes four holes up and our match is over – we are now just completing our round for 'fun' although it is not fun for me at all. I am angry and fed up. I want to stick something to him and so I start throwing out morsels of information about me and with a strategy in mind.

I announce that I have four children to his two. This makes me more virile or foolhardy? Nowadays, four kids is usually of interest and at last, he chucks me a crumb. His first mistake…

What ages? He asks, barely interested.

My eldest is 20.

'Oh, and which university is he at?' he asked. It's a loaded question and yet I welcome it and I sense an opening.

'No. He didn't go to university.'

He processes this and I imagine him ruminating on just how stupid my son must be not to gain a place at university.

'He's an actor.' I added casually, carefully setting out my trap.

His disdain is now apparent. Did I hear a tut. A wastrel, you mean?

'And is he working at the moment? Or is he resting?' he asks.

Our conversation is developing nicely. My golf is forgotten and finally I am enjoying myself.

'Yes. He's in America… making a film…'

At this, his demeanour alters a little. His interest is definitely piqued. So many actors these days hail from the gilded schools and Oxbridge and maybe his kids even gave it a go.

'Really. Anything I might see?'

'No, I expect not. Not your thing. Unless your grandchildren drag you along.'

He registers this but I can't risk him not asking me to expand. And so, I push on.

'It's a film called Homecoming. He plays a character called Peter Parker.'

What now follows is a thing of exquisite beauty and timing because Judge Chinless Fancy Pants has just teed up his ball – and metaphorically it is there for me to smash down the middle of the fairway…

The name Peter Parker meant nothing to him and he shook his head.

Just as he appeared to enjoy not knowing who I was, it was the same for Tom's film and his famous character.

'No,' I begin. 'But you've heard of Spider-Man, right?'

BOOM.

And on the 17th hole, for the first time all day, he hits a shit drive.

I lost the golf but I won the war.

Take Nine

The Impossible Cost of Having Kids

Much is made of the financial costs of having children but not enough weight is ever given to the emotional burden, especially pertaining to having boys, which is all I have.

And such emotional strains can come in ways you least expect. Like when little boys suddenly develop a passion for basketball and I do not mean the inevitable disappointment that they are never going to play in the NBA.

On the basis of their parents stature alone, it is unlikely that basketball is a sport that my boys will ever play in adulthood but this doesn't mean that they can't enjoy the game. And for this to happen a hoop is required at home and this is when the emotional torture begins.

Basketball and a nice garden are completely incompatible. The ball itself is heavy and aggressive. Its surface is abrasive. A basketball from height can flatten any shrub and even take out small trees. Pets should be kept indoors and toddlers too. Even paving slabs will eventually submit to the pounding of the dimpled destroyer. And loud, so unbelievably loud. A basketball will destroy any peace, quiet and everything in its path and this includes the hoop and the net it is supposed to pass through.

Our first hoop was designed to be wall mounted and it was my task to fix it to our house. It came with some heavy industrial fixings, an indication of the punishment it would need to withstand and in due course, having been pounded from all directions, the hoop hung limply and was pulling my kitchen wall away with it.

A ban on basketball was imposed but ignored when my eldest son (with means of his own) decided to buy a new hoop and this time the free-standing variety, complete with pole and base that is filled with water and is the size of a small car.

A financial saving then but one which pales against the high emotional tariff.

It must have been a dark day for my neighbours either side as the hoop appeared mid-garden and they prepared themselves for incoming.

My garden is strewn in cardboard but this is of no concern. Dads do recycling. Everyone knows this. It's one of life's rules. My boys do, however, take complete responsibility for the erection and as it nears completion I notice a number of unused nuts and bolts lying about the place. It is just a matter of time. Tom mutters something about a ten-year guarantee which is a scam. Such a guarantee is only granted because no dad is ever going to be able to return such a monstrosity to a blinking shop?

It's definitely going to break. As night follows day, a basketball hoop cannot withstand the unrelenting punishment.

The ball smashes and crashes against the hoop and occasionally through it. The net is nylon but against the British winter it will quickly start to break down and other parts will follow. The backboard will start to lean. The hoop will droop like my spirits and then one day, my boys will simply lose interest and move on to something else.

And with this, peace resumes. The shrubs have a chance again and all is well?

Well no, not really because the hoop remains. Unused and unloved, a monstrosity that overwhelms my moderately-sized London garden. But discarding it is a job in itself, to dismantle and somehow cram in to my car and then get to the dump with all the emotional baggage that is entailed with adding to landfill.

For now, it remains a constant on my to-do list. Three of my boys are financially independent now but believe me their emotional scars endure. The hoop is a reminder of such and so maybe it has a purpose after all.

Take Ten

Who Lives in a House Like This?

Property porn is a thing now. There is a show on Netflix featuring the world's most desirable homes which I have not watched and nor do I intend to. Not that I don't admire a nice house. Like everyone else when I walk through the more salubrious boroughs of London, my eye is taken by the beautiful drums on show. Often properties adorned with blue plaques to indicate famous previous residents. And I wonder who might live there today and what the hell they do for a living. Banking most likely, or old money? Nice one, Grandad.

In general, we are more admiring if wealth has been made. We respond to the rags to riches fairy-tale and speaking of which, a famous comedian friend of mine lives locally. He bought a wreck of a property and when its renovation was complete he wanted to celebrate with a house warming party and why not?

Er... because ordinary hard-working comedians might not wish to realise that their former comedy club colleague now lives in a freaking palace. Not far from an actual palace (Hampton Court), his house has turrets and a garden so big that his five a side football pitch and swimming pool cannot be seen from the house. He certainly wouldn't need to worry about a disused basketball hoop. (see *Take* Nine)

A summer party, so gazebo like Bedouin tents complete with thick carpets and large sofas had been set up, erected for guests to lounge about in and possibly console themselves.

Naturally, the garden lets on to the river Thames and has its own private mooring. A great opportunity then for any comedians unable to cope, to throw themselves in and have done with it. He happens to be a lovely chap and crucially he is an extremely good comedian and well worth his success. But this kind of success? Really? And this must have occurred to him and why he had St. John's ambulance on standby to deal with any dislocated lower jaws. It's the sort of house I would expect someone like Peter Gabriel or Sir Michael Caine to reside in. As Nikki and I strolled the grounds and took it all in, I suddenly felt an urge to say something. I leaned forward and I whispered gently in to her ear, that I was sorry.

Again, close to where we live is a famously beautiful house made even more famous when Brad Pitt and Angelina Jolie rented it during an extended visit to London. Called The Old House, it is a particularly beautiful home which I used to spy as a young man from the top of a London bus on its way from Richmond. And when it came on the market many years ago, I even called up the estate agent to request the sales particulars.

A plush brochure duly arrived with stunning photography and prose designed to sell the house. £2.5m at the time, so this will tell you just how long ago this was. I never forgot something that was mentioned in the particulars. It made me laugh then and still does today.

"Eight rest rooms in total, all with low-level WC's"

Presumably everything in the house particulars is designed to entice and snare a buyer to make an offer. As though, the house itself with its manicured grounds and wonderful location are not enough. Even the toilets (WC's) are a selling feature and who knows, might just be the difference.

Because these are low level toilets, meaning our bottom is below our knees and the ideal squat position to evacuate ones' bowels. Almost no pushing required with these toilets.

Really?

"…a beautiful home, ideal for people with weak sphincter muscles or people who are just unbelievably lazy. Your waste will slide out like a jellied eel."

Of course, this sounds ridiculous but so does bothering to include low-level WC. As though such a thing warrants mentioning.

"…when we first saw the house, we weren't convinced. But it was the toilets that got us over the line. Low level, you see. Hopefully you'll need a poo after dinner and you can see for yourself."

One thing though on the sales details was omitted.

"Handily located for local buses."

People who can afford such a home, might appreciate a low-level WC but they'd never stoop so low to ever take the bus.

Take Eleven

A Guilty Secret

Some things in life are sacrosanct.

Like disabled parking bays; as tempting as they are with their fiendishly convenient locations. But there can be no excuses. None of the following…

I was in a rush.

I was only a minute.

There were no other spaces.

But there are loads of disabled bays. Look, one, two, three… EIGHT! And next to a gym. What are the odds of eight disabled gym attendees arriving at the same time…

There can be no excuses.

We can never justify parking in a disabled bay and depriving a disabled person easy access to McDonalds. Wrong on so many levels and not something anyone with any sense of decency would countenance.

But that said, using a disabled toilet…

Anyone else?

And I wonder why this is?

I have decided that it is because leaving a car in a disabled parking bay elicits a fine but using a disabled toilet, carries only the risk of being scowled at.

And so, disabled facilities are my preferred toilets. My toilets of choice. So hallowed, they are often locked but as yet I have never dared limp over to a kiosk to request a key.

So many advantages of the disabled toilet. To begin with, they are large and with space to move around. A chance to take off a jacket easily and even hang it up. The locks on the door work which is welcome. Very often they are private, too. The cubicles are contained and we cannot be overheard. And in my experience, the disabled toilets are always cleaner and tidier than the non-disabled toilets, an indictment for the so-called able-bodied users with their loose bowels and filthy habits.

All welcome advantages and as if these are not enough, some disabled toilets even provide back rests also. I have never felt an urge to recline when sitting on a toilet. Quite the opposite in fact, I like to lean forward but each to their own.

The only issue is leaving the toilet of course and hoping that people are not waiting in line. People who are more eligible to use it and ready with their best scowl. Which no one enjoys receiving but it will always be preferable to a fine and so I am afraid, it will always be a risk worth taking.

Take Twelve

Man on Fire

Some men play golf. Some men play football. Some men fish and some play piano. Others write poetry and I daresay some men even knit or crochet.

But all men BBQ.

And I think I am right in saying, all men.

Something deep in our marrow and our carnal instincts. A nod to our ancestry when most men hunted and a minority gathered.

An instinct that is rekindled the moment meat needs to be cooked in the garden.

Salads, rice and anything else to accompany the burnt meats are prepared inside the house and this remains largely the preserve of the female of our species.

And to complete this cliché, the man on 'meat' duty will often stand with a beer in hand as other men gather around the fire and marvel at the scene before them. This gathering is itself very unusual. No men have ever huddled around an indoor oven while a chicken is being roasted.

But a BBQ has an extraordinary allure. Like moths to a flame or flies to a dog turd, men will marvel at the outdoor cooker.

Some men might offer their help because most men think they can do it better. That they have some meat burning wisdom to impart. They might even suggest that they take over the flipping for a while.

But such offers are never welcome and are always rebuffed. No self-respecting man ever gives up meat burning duties at his own BBQ.

'Thanks pal, but no thanks. You've got more chance getting hold of my wife than you have my tongs.'

And this annual ritual of male bonding is not undermined by the ease of modern day living. Few of us hunt our food these days, unless we go to one of those massive hangar-like supermarkets where it is so easy to get lost and we need to be rescued.

We have no need for flints and kindling anymore to create the magic of fire. Now that we have gas bottles and ignition switches which mostly work, for the first season at least. And beyond this, it really depends on whether the BBQ can be squeezed in to the shed for the winter.

Cooking outdoors is the carefree lifestyle we all hanker for. Often, the food we buy comes already marinated and so the BBQ taste is equally achieved by using the oven. But this is to miss the point. Cooking inside is bland and boring. Cooking outside is always fun and always exciting.

There are hurdles to overcome...

The weather can turn. It can start to rain, but so what? Undeterred, all men have BBQ'd huddled under umbrellas emblazoned with PING and CALLAWAY.

The food is also highly likely to burn and char. But so what?

GOOD.

It is supposed to burn. "I am cooking on an open fire. What do you expect?"

Very often, the food will burn to a point of being unrecognisable and it then needs to be scraped. Again, all part of the fun especially when someone approaches the hot zone with a plate of salad and rice and utters the immortal words;

'Vegetarian sausages please?'

Blimey, good luck. Everything is burnt and looks the same.

And if this isn't funny at the time, then it will be later on when the guests have gone home.

Take Thirteen

Apple Crumble

My professional life is a simple one.

I make people laugh for money. An unusual transaction and not really an essential one. Not like being a surgeon, or a farmer. But there is demand for laughs and since I have jokes and stories…

But this does not mean that my professional life is not complex.

And fiendishly complex when it comes to writing and publishing my own books (this one included). Book publishing and book selling requires me to fully embrace technology and this is not a strong suit of mine and so, my wife, Nikki suggested I attend an IT course.

She booked me on to a session at our local Apple store and I duly went along.

Having four children, I might have realised that my appointment was during half term and that cunning parents might be looking for ways to offload their out-of-school children and for free.

Arriving at the store in good time, it has just opened and is largely empty. Just the staff standing round, all tattoos and beany hats – but for one table in the corner which is full of young children already. And with one spare seat.

My spirits plummet but I don't have time for embarrassment. My book sales are on the line and I am mustard keen in a way that I never was at school.

As a class, we make an odd site. I look like an incredibly slow learner or a deviant, neither of which is a great look. I'm a little paranoid, and when the pushy mums' arrive at the end of class to pick up their brats I spy some awkward glances.

I smile and I try to assure them; IT'wise I am slow but I am certainly not a nonce and I have no tendencies in this area whatever. And I can prove this if needs be because I have with me my laptop – and anyone is welcome to browse my hard drive. Nothing to see here. My browsing history is not even deleted. I have nothing to hide. Indeed, the only thing on my laptop that is embarrassing are my book sales and this is the reason why I am present in a class with a bunch of kids.

Then my wife arrives to pick me up. I tell the teacher thank you and I present to him a gift. An apple obviously…

Take Fourteen

A Hero Amongst us…

Brain surgeons along with rocket scientists are the professions used to denote intelligence. Understandably so, we admire such professionals. Fiendishly clever and pioneers in their field. At school, I couldn't understand physics at all. Inertia, momentum, gravity and energy… it was all impossible to me and so the idea of Astro-Physics; the study of physics not on earth, but in space is completely unfathomable.

It's not rocket science…

A phrase we are all familiar with. Used to indicate how simple something is. Although I imagine that this phrase is seldom heard in NASA HQ because what they actually do, really is rocket science.

Recently I had lunch with an eminent brain surgeon but not in a professional capacity. Not his anyway, thank God. In fact he was a paediatric brain surgeon and so unaccustomed to working on brains as large as mine.

And we were not alone for lunch. It was not just the two of us.

We were joined by one hundred and twenty other people. The occasion was a fundraiser for the world-famous Great Ormond Street Hospital and the venue was a super expensive hotel. Not a problem for the people gathered, as wealthy and successful as they are.

The car park is stiff with expensive cars. And I note that three helicopters have landed on a driving range on an adjoining golf course. It occurs to me that if anything is going to incentivise a struggling golfer, then it is taking aim at a billionaire's helicopter.

Sitting opposite the surgeon, what strikes me about him is his modesty. In the programme for the dinner is his potted biography and I note he conducts over two hundred operations a year. That's an extraordinary number of ill children and also I imagine the pressure on him, being responsible for the lives and hopes of so many children and their parents.

He and I bond further - not in our relative poverty but in our strange jobs. He refers to our professions as career choices. He puts it kindly, suggesting that we chose different paths. I nod in agreement but in truth I don't recall that brain surgery was ever an option for me.

I asked him if his job ever becomes routine - and he pauses for a moment to reflect and then replies, 'no, not really.' Ahead of an operation, he explained that he is always heightened and anxious. As though he knows that something is askew and he is about to do something out of the ordinary – like open a child's cranium and mooch about in their brain.

Which is exactly how I feel during lunch because once puddings are done with and coffee is down, I am expected to stand up and make the whole room laugh.

The surgeon smiles at me. A smile that says rather you than me.

Ditto mate, I say with my smile in return.

I don't really do awe. Certainly not for show-biz people anyway because I know the part that luck plays in this arena. Sports stars are easier for me to admire because I can't do what they can and the same applies to a world leading neuro-surgeon.

The money raised on the day was enormous and credit to the people who paid for auction lots, many of which I expect will never be redeemed.

Wealth is certainly a barometer of life. Something tangible and easy to gauge and compare. And admired too. I am always amused by how salacious stories in the press are accompanied by the value of the house where the marriage ending trysts occurred.

But wealth is not always a reliable indicator of worth.

In the room that day, there were many big hitters. I mulled this over during our lunch, trying to create a suitable opening line for my speech – something flattering and galvanising but also comic and impactful. And I settled on something like…

'Here we are in a room full of big hitters. Captains of industry. Dare-I-say-it, but today I stand amongst some enormous big swinging dicks – and you know who you are. But that said, I think we can all agree who the real Silver Back is amongst us – it is the man sitting here who happens to save kid's lives for a living…'

They clapped their hands and roared their approval. And they spent big. God bless 'em, the filthy rich bastards.

Take Fifteen

IQ/EQ

School fund raisers are a big thing nowadays. Good for the school and for the parents too for forging friendships and relationships. But more fun for some parents than others, for instance when the fundraiser is a comedy evening and one parent happens to be a comedian.

Most comedians prefer not to do gigs to people they know. Too risky that they might chance upon a smelly gig which we all have from time to time. That tough crowd, the drunk heckler, the cold room, poor sound…

Doing The Comedy Store in London used to attract lots of my friends and family and this always ramped up the pressure even more. One weekend, my entire street booked tickets and I said to Nikki, 'Blimey, a bad gig tonight and we're gonna have to move house.'

So performing at your kids school is definitely off-limits for most comedians and often at the child's insistence.

But this is a bullet I have failed to dodge. I have been roped in on many occasions. At least ten gigs and counting. Hosting dinners. After dinner speeches and flat out comedy evenings, with me usually hosting. When my boys were in primary school I hosted a school ball at Sandown Park Race Course. After the event, a dad I didn't know approached me full of exuberance.

'Blimey. You were so funny. You could be a bloody comedian.'

But there is a school fundraiser that I dread even more than the comedy night and it is, of course, the school quiz.

School is a highly competitive environment and so it should be, because so is life. Which kid is top of the class? Who is cast to play Danny or Sandy in Greece? A team, B team or no team…

And now this competition extends to the parents also with a blinking quiz and some parents take it very seriously indeed. In full boot camp training a few weeks out studying capital cities, oceans, populations and works of literature.

Not me though. I can't be bothered. I will wait for the sport questions and chip in elsewhere where I can. And I will clap the winning table and remark what a predictable win it was.

Intelligence is highly prized. It is a good gauge of success that might lie ahead but not always.

At a family gathering, (it was actually my dad's funeral and wake) a man had been speaking with my eldest son and afterwards he was keen to speak with me.

'Are you not worried that he has not been to university? And he doesn't have a degree.'

An unusual question and statement which I parried out of politeness and because of the occasion also.

'But his education is incomplete.' The man continued.

I looked at him now, a little oddly. I had never met him before and I didn't know his name. A friend from my parents church I think. And us being Catholics, I would say he was probably Sri Lankan. But I didn't ask, obviously.

I am patient though. Clearly, he has no idea what Tom does for a living and that his not having a degree is unlikely to impede him.

But then he floors me with…

'Anyway, I have two young sons. They're huge fans of Spider-Man and I would like to know when can your son come to my house to have pizza with them?'

Really?

Formal and academic intelligence is important but so is emotional intelligence and sometimes it is a better indicator of the life that lies ahead.

Take Sixteen

Care for a Walk?

A sure sign of ageing is ranting and shouting at the news. Being irked by a news bulletin announcing that some numpty hill walkers have been airlifted to safety.

Hill walking in February. Didn't they check the weather? Air lifted!

"How much did that cost? And more importantly, who paid for it? I'll tell who paid for it…" I find myself muttering to myself.

Over the years I have met many explorer types. Surely, being an 'explorer' is one of the most dubious professions of all. Even more ill-fangled than being a life coach. Explorer is a first world profession if ever there is one and exclusively the preserve of the privileged.

Kids from ordinary backgrounds might dream of heading to the North Pole but for how many is this ever an option?

And redundant because of course, it's been done already, the Poles I mean. And so are they really exploring at all? This is why they need to dream up ever increasing hardships for missions already completed. The first posh man to walk to the North Pole wearing flip flops.

Completing an arduous task hopefully with some tangible injuries and scarring for the inevitable book release and forthcoming conference speeches.

Motivational speeches is what these chaps deliver at conferences to unsuspecting sales reps of various companies. Although quite what a double-glazing salesman can learn from a bloke called Piers who sailed the Atlantic in a bathtub is beyond me.

These motivational speeches take place during the day and I have sat through enough of them to know that they are basically all the same.

Be determined. Believe in yourself. Do your best. Enjoy the highs and learn from the lows. Never give up. Surround yourself with good people…

Sports stars do very nicely giving practically the same speech as each other. Same jokes but with players names changed.

Ranulph Fiennes is the king of the motivational speakers. He has walked to both Poles and has the missing digits to prove it – and on show when the punters finally get to the head of the queue waiting to have their book signed.

Don't get me wrong, I admire fortitude and bravery and especially so since I am not tough at all. Not by any measure. I put comfort above all else and I seek to avoid pain wherever possible.

But when I sit at the back of a conference room and listen to a Rupert or a Henry talk about their hard and grinding walk,

I am slightly resentful and for two reasons. Firstly, because later on in the evening this sober audience will be drunk and if my speech is received with the same silence, then the client is likely to question my invoice. But also because the walk they are describing is not so difficult and in fact, I have done harder walks myself. And I put it to you, that you have too.

Most of us have. Most of us have completed harder walks than getting to either magnetic Pole. I hope that you're intrigued now because I am about to reveal what this walk is. The walk that you might well have already completed.

The hardest walk on earth is…

…the walk down the stairs from the top diving board.

Take Seventeen

Relaxing at Sea

Cruising the Mediterranean with my family is a costly pursuit. Looking at the sea where migrants are chancing everything for a better life as we float about in opulence is an emotional strain as well as a big financial hit. We could only afford a week.

But it is all-inclusive and so as I board, I can finally relax.

Or can I?

Because some drinks are included but not all. Some activities too. And definitely not the arcade games. Plus the ship stops off at tourist hotspots and we are greeted ashore by adoring locals with visa machines.

And yet as beautiful as Pisa is and Pompeii is fascinating, it seems to me that food is the central focus of the cruise ship and an area where the Holland family felt most ripped off. Because we can't eat ALL the food that is on offer and so we are effectively subsidising those patrons who evidently can.

The most important job on a cruise ship is not the Captain.

But the person charged with budgeting and calculating the all-inclusive price points. It must be a minefield. Get it wrong and profits are sunk. A ship full of committed eaters is a very heavy and expensive load. And just like their jogging bottoms, the profit margins are tight.

But how to budget and discern what levels of food to provide. Presumably online booking forms cannot ask for such sensitive information.

"Ticking the following boxes, how would you describe your appetite?"

Five boxes, graduating from moderate eater to glutton?

Perhaps, such sensitive information could be gleaned under the guise of Health and Safety and life boat provision by requesting passengers height and weight.

Or perhaps the fairest way to price a cruise is to ask passengers to pay at the end of the voyage – and everyone is weighed on embarking and then again on disembarking. This prospect might thin the lines of people for the midnight eat-all-you-can pizza buffet.

On the ship, the food is magnificent. Stored in the bowels of the vessel, cooked, prepared and served by legions of people from the Philippines and India it seems and adding to the emotional toll and the notion of privilege.

Not to say though that cruising is stress free with many passengers facing the constant conundrum of how to be sufficiently hungry in time for the next meal. Goldfish are often criticized for being so stupid that given enough food, they will eat themselves to death.

Well…

On our ship there were plenty of passengers no more intelligent than our favourite domestic fish and often they were the same colour too.

For most of us, food is the best part of the day. It is what we look forward to. What shall we eat tonight? Holidays are often ranked on how good the food is.

Which brings me to another cherished pastime of walking.

We can all think of our favourite walks. On the beach. Through the woods. On the hill tops. Through little villages or across the big city.

And as beautiful and as invigorating as these walks are, I put it to you that these are not the best walks of all.

Think about what this walk might be.

Some clues for you…

The best walk of all is relatively short. It is usually in a circle. Often two laps of the same grid. And it is full of excitement.

I give you…

The first walk around the buffet island.

Take Eighteen

Creature Comforts

Some men are more 'manly' than others.

This is a fact but not a very comfortable one these days.

Define manly, is a question to keep most of us quiet because our answers are bound to exclude some people and offend others.

But you know what I mean? You know what I am inferring?

That a manly man is tough, gritty, hard, hairy, smelly perhaps, brave...

And these are qualities that we admire. These are the qualities of a man's man. Or a He-Man. Although this term feels very outdated and dangerous. A pronoun disaster and on its own, probably enough for a Ph.D. from the University of North East Luton.

Anyway, my point is this... however we refer to them, such men are unlikely to be interested in being comfortable. And I don't mean comfortably off. By comfortable, I mean being disposed to pyjamas, slippers, velour's and corduroys.

This is very much where I live. And if this makes me unmanly, then fine, I am comfortable with that.

Even as a little boy I sought out comfort. And now as a little man, I still do.

To this day, as soon as I get home, my first job is to locate my slippers; not easy because our dog loves my slippers even more than me and constantly makes off with them. My solution to this is to have multiple pairs of slippers and a willingness to mix and match. I don't care if this makes me look like a lunatic. I don't even mind wearing two right slippers or two lefts and from different pairs, just so long as my feet are wrapped in wool.

One pair I currently have on the go are too small for me. They were in the sale and I bought them because the sales assistant assured me that they would stretch. But they didn't. And so they need to be prised on and off which is not terribly relaxing and rather undermines their purpose.

Recently in Marks and Spencer which is an unmanly shop and happens to be one of my favourites, I spied a shoe horn and it immediately appealed. Particularly so because it was a very long shoe horn. A horn that enables the user to avoid bending over whilst pulling on a shoe.

We choose a lot of things in life, including the people to share our lives with. And on this subject, let's be honest here, that if relationships are to last, then compromises are called for.

'I wish you'd make more of an effort.'

These are words that I hear from my wife (life partner?) on a fairly regular basis and it usually pertains to how I dress. Because once again, comfort is paramount and trumps aesthetics every time. This is a crime to my wife. Recently I was chastised for wearing a green shirt with a pair of brown jeans – and my answer was not well received.

'It seems to work for trees.'

But I see her point and it's an important one. What she is asking for is not unreasonable and it is in my interest also. That she wants to find me attractive. Presumably, she fancied me once and she wants this to continue.

With this in mind, allow me to set a scene for you.

The other morning, I needed to leave two empty milk bottles outside our front door. So my wife had the ignominy of seeing the man she had chosen, in his pyjamas and using a shoe horn to pull on his slippers.

That's a tough thing for any wife to witness.

In truth, I figure that Nikki settled on a husband rather than chose one. She probably hoped that I might improve or that she might be able to mould me.

An ongoing challenge then, and one that she will lose.

Take Nineteen

The Real Cost of a Holiday.

The real cost of a holiday is not the price of the trip but the stress of returning home. The anxiety of getting back to real life. And hopefully to work.

And other anxieties too.

Have we been burgled, always ranks high.

Burst pipes? (skiing)

Did we leave the iron on?

Or hair straighteners? (my wife, not me).

The fridge will stink.

And what about the mail that will be waiting for me as I try to push open my front door. This will need to be sorted in to piles by name and importance…

My favourite pile of letters are the circulars that don't need to be opened and can be thrown out immediately. Letters from charities, some of whom we already support but who want more - and others from new causes who we might like to support.

"Enjoy your holiday, did you? These kids in India are going blind…"

Then there is always a further pile of official looking letters. Some in brown envelopes with address windows and adorned in bold – IMPORTANT and HMRC. This is my least favourite pile and despite being IMPORTANT - I usually ignore it for another week or so.

There is little good news from the postman nowadays. The days of receiving unexpected cheques are over. I have premium bonds but never in my life…

On the flight home, I wonder if like me, everyone else on the plane is fretting and making lists? A to-do list to ease back in to life. Often headed by lay off the booze for a while.

As soon as the plane lands, the rush is on. To disembark and get through immigration. My fame level has receded such that I am rarely recognised nowadays which I don't mind at all. But in this instance I do want to be recognised because I have selected the passport machine instead of a comatose customs official.

My entry to the UK and my ego rests then on a machine – as I wait with my passport in the slot, hoping it will recognise me.

Come on, I say quietly and hopefully.

It's me!

Have I Got News For You, perhaps?

The Royal Variety Show…

The machine takes a long time before it finally grants me entry. Almost begrudgingly. As though the machine is saying , "… haven't seen you on telly for years mate."

But finally I am through and now facing one of the most depressing places on earth; the baggage carousel. Stilted and hushed conversations as we wait for the belt to trundle into life. Whose bag will be first? Mine will be last. Bound to be. Always is…

"Look, that bag has been around three times already. Where the fuck are these people…"

It's a wait in stark contrast to the exciting wait at the airport on your outbound journey. Waiting for bags containing your best clothes all cleaned, ironed and ready to go.

Heathrow, two weeks later. A different story.

Waiting for your dirty washing.

Three loads at least.

Have we even got washing powder? And we'll need to stop and get milk…

Take Twenty

Fading Stars

I was a youngster when Madonna exploded in to so many of our lives. *Holiday* was her pop anthem that captivated the world. That voice of hers, so childlike, and yet she is somehow a grown adult and possibly the sexiest woman alive. It was all a heady combination and the decades ahead firmly belonged to her. Hit songs interspersed with mild pornography, short forays into film and even shorter marriages kept Madge in the newspapers and riding high.

But by the time I joined the throng to watch her at Wembley Stadium, her allure was waning and by her encore, for me it had all but vanished. Another baby-voiced siren had arrived called Kylie but by then I understood that Yamaha and not a larynx or voice box was responsible for the sound. Kylie beguiled the world when she sang, *I should be so lucky* and still famous in 2020, how apocryphal this was.

But even when infamy continues, fame tends to dwindle.

Tom was in America to present an Oscar and at one of the post-ceremony parties, he was introduced to Madonna. And because his lip-synch battle mimicking Rhianna and her umbrella had gone viral, the person who introduced Tom did so as a great dancer. Madonna appeared unimpressed or at least she needed proof. So she asked Tom to show her some moves. The poor lad, reluctantly he complied. Moves to accompany his squirms, I imagine.

The next day, Tom called home. To catch up in general and to hear about normal family life. Our news might be mundane but it seems to anchor him still.

Naturally, we were keen to hear about his brush with Oscar and he began to share his anecdote from the party.

As I frequently do with Tom's life, I relate it to my own. An abiding memory of mine is walking to school for an A Level biology class. Always exciting since biology was studied at a girls school which played a major role in me choosing the subject. A chance to hopefully practise biology as well as study it. At the time, my most prized possession was my Sony Walkman and I recall blasting *Holiday* in to my headphones as I headed to the girls school with everything crossed. To think then that some 30 years later my son would be dancing with the girl in my ears.

Anyway, back to the story.

On speaker phone now, Tom continues with his tale and much hilarity ensues. But the biggest laugh is yet to come, because also listening to Tom's story was his youngest brother, Patrick. But he didn't share our excitement and nor did he understand why this story was even noteworthy.

'Who's Madonna?' he asked.

Ouch.

Take Twenty-One

Ego Check

A few years ago and we are on our way to watch the tennis at the Wimbledon Championships.

We didn't win a ballot. We hadn't even entered. We didn't have tickets but we did have Tom and he gets invited to these kind of events.

The stadium is not far from our house, just a short train ride but they sent a car anyway. Thanks very much. In to the pristine grounds of Wimbledon and quickly we are whisked to a hospitality lounge. Tom is asked for a photograph by Sam Torrance, the golfer who captained the winning Ryder Cup Team, held the winning putt in a Ryder Cup as a player and has won 44 professional events. It wasn't that long ago that I was teaching a young Tom to play golf and to contain his tantrums, so you will understand why this photo request felt surreal to me. I held Mr Torrance's coat as I remember.

At the time, *Spider-Man Far From Home* is riding high at the Box Office. Tom's life is changing rapidly and as his dad, I am very protective of him and hankering after how things were and hoping that things might remain normal.

But this is unlikely.

Tom is visible now. His face is on buses and billboards and walking about the Championships, heads are turning. People double take. They confer with each other and when they agree that it is him, sometimes they call out his name. Some people ask for photos but thankfully not many.

Tom is becoming famous. A cost of his success?

People are excited to see him and even more so when it is out of context and unexpected. But my parental DNA is always to protect him. Come on guys, leave him alone. He's just an ordinary kid, albeit doing some extraordinary things. But even so, nothing to see here. Move along…

On the way out of the Championships, the streets are busy and we are trying to meet the car that is waiting for us. Tom is charging ahead of me, a metaphor for our diverging lives. And Nikki is some way behind (sore feet). A bunch of exuberant lads are ahead. As we pass, one lad spots Tom.

"Bloody hell, that's Spider-Man."

A cheer goes up and then immediately a jeer because the guy is not believed by his buddies. Tom doesn't break stride. And as I pass the lads, I hear a general conflab…

"That bloke there. I'm serious, that's Spider-Man."

"No, way… you're full of shit."

"I'm telling you. I've just seen his movie, Far From Home. That geezer is…"

I risk a glance backwards – hoping that they're not giving chase – and still emitting my 'leave him alone' energy of a protective dad.

Their back and forth continues, some distance back now but I can still hear.

"Up there… that is Tom Holland."

"Who's Tom Holland?"

And this stops me.

What?

Protective dad replaced immediately by indignant dad.

Who is Tom Holland?

Are you serious?

Graham Norton three times. Billboards. Sides of buses. 5 movies as the web slinger…

Ladies and gentlemen, I present to you, the ego. A thing we all possess and we must always be mindful to keep in check.

Take Twenty-Two

Rowing is Backwards

We all know where we stand in the world of sport. Even if we don't play sports anymore, we know how we rank by drawing on our school days.

A team? B team? No team? Picked first or last at break-time?

Like my academics, my sporting prowess was unremarkable. Solid B team footballer. Technically, I was a good footballer but I was too small and not pushy enough to trouble the A team and my hopelessly late development didn't help much either.

And yet because of my size I could have become an Olympian.

Our PE teacher was a certain Mr Martin Cross. Ring any bells? No, probably not. But Mr Cross won an Olympic gold medal in the 1984 games in the coxed fours with some bloke called Steven Redgrave. Mr Cross brought his medal in for us to purr over and suddenly our school embraced rowing. Calling all tall boys who can't play football. Rowing became a great refuge for the lanky dispossessed sportsmen.

You may know that a rowing boat needs more than just tall oarsmen. It needs a cox. Preferably a small kid to steer the boat and this is where I come in. More astute readers will have gathered already that I was honoured to be asked to be the school cox. Only it didn't feel like much of an honour. In fact, I was mortally offended. Me, steer a bloody boat. But I'm a midfield general. B team captain, no less.

There was no one else suitable (small enough) in my year and so the rowers looked to the year below and managed to snare the services of Gary Herbert who is now the voice of BBC rowing and commentating brilliantly I might add. When we all urged Redgrave over the line in Beijing, there wasn't a dry British eye watching and much of this was down to Gary's impassioned commentary.

But I couldn't have known at the time that in saying no to rowing that I was foregoing a career as a BBC commentator. I carried on marshalling my B team football side whilst Gary enjoyed considerably more success in his rowing boat. But so what? Who wants to be a bloody cox?

Gary did.

And he ended up being the cox for the Searle brothers, names you might be familiar with. Jonny and Greg to be exact, the brothers who grabbed gold in the 1992 Barcelona Olympics with Gary at their steering wheel. The first I knew about this was watching it unfold on television. A tiny head at the end of the boat, Gary wasn't recognisable but then I heard his name mentioned by the race commentator and I began to wonder. Could this be the same Gary Herbert I had been at school with? It had to be, surely? Not such a common name, especially Gary. Only Lineker and Glitter being the other Gary's in the whole of the UK.

At the end of one of their qualifying heats, Gary emerged from the boat in celebration and indeed, it was the very same. Blimey. Gary is an Olympian and he was the second-choice cox as well, after me.

Suddenly I became very interested in the Searle Brothers and their progress. And I roared them on.

Come on Greg. Come on Jonny. Row hard. Pull hard. Pull… And Gary also, keep steering!

Could they win I wondered and how would I feel, knowing that it could have been me in the boat?

With the rest of the country I cheered the boys as they duly won Gold. Gary was an Olympic gold medallist. Blimey. How's the football career going, Dom?

And then something happened that I have never forgotten and still makes me laugh to this day. During the medal ceremony, the Union Jack was being raised as God Save the Queen rang out, the camera closed in on Greg Searle. A granite jawed hunk, seemingly unmoved by the occasion. The camera then moved across horizontally to his equally stoic and enormous brother. The two of them, a study in masculinity. And then the camera moved down vertically by a couple of feet and then across to grab a shot of the comparatively diminutive Gary Herbert, who happened to be blubbing his eyes out.

And in this moment, I didn't feel any regret at all. I felt only relief. Thank God, I had said no.

Gold medal aside.

I didn't want to be the on the podium next to two giants and be the only one not out of breath.

Take Twenty-Three

Squeeze for the Camera

The Mayor of London, Sadiq Khan does it a lot. David Beckham too and Joseph Gordon Levitt. A whole raft of show-biz types in fact, including on occasion and to my horror, my eldest son.

I refer to the pulling of a certain face for the cameras. Ben Stiller called it Blue Steele in his movie Zoolander, but I think this pose is slightly different.

It involves the narrowing of the eyes and adopting a subtle and general strain to the face. To me, it's a look that says, "Hey, I'm sexy. Have you noticed?"

It might be classically described as 'the smoulder' but I think a more accurate description is the 'doing a poo' look.

As I say in the introduction, this book is designed to be read in toilets and so presumably some readers might well be doing this look whilst reading this *Take* and if so, I salute you.

A previous Mayor of London is currently the Prime Minister of Great Britain and no doubt the ambitious Mr Khan would love to repeat this career path. Hence his 'doing a poo' look in all his publicity shots to capture our votes and hopefully the top gig in years to come. But this is a tall order.

Under his Mayorship, the old roads of London have been butchered to make way for hundreds of miles of cycle lanes – and because we are British and not Dutch, none of these cycle lanes are being used. Where I live, the newly installed cycle lanes are shunned for being too perilous; having to accommodate bus stops and trapping general detritus to tip cyclists off too easily.

Meanwhile, the remaining constricted roads are much more congested. Journey times are longer. Emissions are up. Cars crammed and crawling next to empty cycle lanes.

Fuel consumption up also along with frustrations. And compounded by the radio advertising campaign (at our expense) extolling the virtues of its transport policy with the catchy slogan...

"To the Mayor of London and Transport for London (TfL), every journey matters."

That is, unless your journey happens to be in a car.

In the movie, Field of Dreams, Kevin Costner was instructed to build the field and the players will come. And they duly did.

The same logic is employed here.

Build the cycle lanes and the cyclists will come.

But will they?

No one would argue against the merits of the bicycle. But in cities as vast as London, when it is dark by 3pm in the winter, wet and cold... how realistic an option is cycling?

The politicians though are determined that this will happen. Cameras at every junction await to charge and fine motorists and squeeze them out of their cars and on to bicycles.

It might work but I doubt it.

A dangerous gamble then. It is not just the many £millions spent on this new infrastructure. It is the political careers of the politicians responsible that is also on the line.

These individuals will be hoping and praying that they will be vindicated. And fretting that their call is wrong. Our London mayor might even be shitting himself and if so, this explains how he looks whenever he sees a camera.

Take Twenty-Four

My BIG Break

To write something worth reading, one needs a good imagination or to be fortunate that things just occur that are worth chronicling.

Recently, my phone rang which these days is quite an occurrence and it took me a little by surprise.

An Unknown Number, I deliberated whether or not to answer.

You know the grating calls that these so often are…

'…hello… we have been advised that you recently had a road traffic accident that was not your fault…'

But I took the call which was a good decision because it happened to be my agent.

Now, you might be wondering how it is that my agent's phone number is unrecognisable to my highly sophisticated mobile phone. In which case, you and me both.

Anyway, cursory pleasantries over, it was down to business and a potential job for me. An acting job no less.

Am I available for dates in Feb, March and possibly beyond…

"Am I?"

I didn't say this, of course. What I said, is that I needed to check my diary and then carefully gauge how long to leave my agent waiting. Enough time to give the impression of a busy man. A piece of 'talent' in high demand. A technique I have honed over the years.

I have had bigger breaks in snooker than I have in acting and so this is an exciting phone call to receive.

I had been requested to audition for a series that will launch a new streaming service for a Goliath media company. A drama that is set to be huge and who knows, quite possibly will be the show-biz breaks for the actors lucky enough to be cast.

The role I am reading for is a school teacher.

The email downloads and I print off the two pages of script that they want me to film myself reading. Or acting, darling.

I read the lines and my confidence grows. Nothing too complicated and certainly within my skill set. I am a father of four and in my book at least, this makes me a teacher. And then something occurs to me. I need to speak to my wife, Nikki because she will know.

Nikki, you know that TV series, the one that Paddy (our youngest) has already been cast in?

Yeah, what about it?

Paddy is playing a school boy, right? Called Monty?

And my suspicions are confirmed. I am auditioning to play the school teacher of my very own son. We all agree that this is funny. But I remain the only one so delusional to think that this could be my big break also.

I rehearse the lines and then I do them with Paddy playing his character and doing his lines back to me. And if I say so myself, I am magnificent. I seize the lines and I own the part. The role is mine, surely. Just the formality of their approval and sign-off. I send the clips in and my wait for confirmation begins.

Nikki and Paddy go back to their lives but mine is on hold, for now.

Anyone who has read my book, *Eclipsed* will know the outcome of this already. But do read on because it has a cruel but funny payoff.

I hear no word by the time Paddy is required to attend a rehearsal day. Nikki took him in to town while I remained at home and continued to rest. I check my phone. Nothing. But, no news is good…

On their return, Paddy is tired but happy and excited. The day went well which is very good news.

'Hey dad, the teacher was there.'

And this is how I find out?

No point in informing Dominic Holland. He'll figure it out, soon enough. But worse was to come when Nikki chips in with,

'The guy they cast as the teacher. He's a right dish.'

Nice. Thanks a lot.

*

To tie up a loose end…

Snooker is a sport that I have played a fair amount of in my time. Although, it is not a game I am emotionally suited to. I get nervous, you see. I remember playing once and being on for a big break. But it was ruined by the prospect of the maximum. As soon as that Hallowed number – 147 – became a possibility, my game collapsed and I missed the next red.

And so to this day, despite my best efforts, my biggest snooker break stands at 8.

Take Twenty-Five

A Local Cold War

Let me set a scene...

The Beast from the East was upon us. A perishing March with the UK experiencing freezing temperatures and feeling the bite of Russian winds. And not just Russian weather to chill us but their politics also. The Salisbury poisoning of a Russian man and his daughter is fresh in our minds and then a further murder of a Russian businessman in a house not a mile from where we live in the capital.

The information on this latest murder victim is hazy. The word being that he has embezzled millions from Aeroflot and his murder was made to look like a suicide. This embezzlement story is undermined by his choice of dwelling; a thirties three bed semi but this is an unnecessary aside and the poor man remains dead.

His house is duly cordoned off with white tents. His house and the ones either side. With a heavy police presence and a lone police officer standing sentry 24 hours a-day in case the murderers return for some evidence that they might have left.

And absolutely freezing cold, the whole thing feels very Russian.

Driving past the house one day and during yet another snow flurry, we remarked on the role of the police officer standing outside and what a short straw he had drawn. When to think he could be in a warm station with a coffee, monitoring nasty tweets for hate crimes.

And then returning home a couple of hours later – and with the weather even worse – the same poor officer remained. Standing ram rod straight, probably because he was frozen solid and from our warm car (heated seats, don't you know) - the moment rather took us...

An impromptu detour to our local train station where I buy a Costa coffee from a machine. Coffee that is never quite hot enough and a chocolate bar from a vending machine. I narrow the chocolate choice down to two options. A *Kit Kat* but I worried that their slogan, *Take a Break* might torment him, and so I go with option two, a *Picnic*. Now with hindsight I think this was a mistake also, because standing in the freezing cold, what this guy was definitely not having, was a picnic.

Excited, we raced back to the scene of the crime discussing the ethics of the situation. Namely, whether or not the police would be allowed to accept such gifts?

Because these are highly unusual circumstances…

We are heading to a Russian murder scene where poison has been implicated and we are intending to give the guard on duty, a cup of coffee.

I make this point and Nikki agrees; it could well be an issue. Nikki dwells on this as we get ever nearer and then hastily suggests that I should be the one to hand it over.

Really, why?

I am driving the car and it was her idea.

Nikki goes quiet now. I can sense her discomfort, despite her bottom being warmed.

Then finally she pipes up…

"No, I can't do it. You'll have to do it. You'll just need to park up and do it."

But why?

"Well…" Nikki begins and then quickly falters. I'm all ears. "… um, er, because he might think that I'm somehow involved. Involved with the murder."

I look at her, oddly.

And are you?

"No, of course I'm not. But he might think I am."

Right. And why would be think that?

"Well. The policeman might think that I am a girlfriend of one of these Russian oligarchs!"

I smile at this.

"Nikki, no offence, but…"

Take Twenty-Six

Table for Two Please

Doing a TV show, I met and got to know a celebrity chef called Anthony Worrell Thompson. He was very famous at the time but since then, his star has perished. During filming, he had a restaurant quite close to where we live in London. He's an amenable chap and we got on very well and he extended an invitation for Nikki and I to dine at his restaurant. Not gratis. Just that he would make sure we would get a table and be well looked after. Thanks very much Anthony. I logged the offer for possible future use.

We all understand that being able to secure a table in a salubrious restaurant is one of the great marks of success.

Scroll forward some months later, maybe even a year and Nikki and I are planning a meal out. Where shall we go? A usual haunt or do we risk somewhere new? And then I recalled my friend who happens to be a famous chef and who has a restaurant close by.

"Try Anthony Worrell Thompson's place." I suggest and I pluck the name of his restaurant from thin air. Nikki scoffs. Bound to be fully booked. But she goes off to do some googling for the number and to make the call.

But no luck. They are fully booked. Disappointing but to be expected. After all, he's a famous chef.

"Did you tell them who I was?" I ask.

A dangerous enquiry and a variation on the always grating,

Do you know who I am?

Nikki heard my question but chose to ignore her stupid and tiresome husband. Of course, she had no idea of its context and my question's validity. That Anthony and I are close personal (show-biz) friends and that I am welcome any time in his eatery. We are fully booked but a discreet table for Mr Dominic Holland… no problem.

And so mischievously I asked her again.

"When you called up for a table. Did you tell them it was me, Dominic Holland?"

Nikki bristles now. And to think that her husband makes a living being funny?

So I ask again.

And her answer is one of the reasons I love her and why we get on so well (mostly).

"Nikki, when you tried to book…"

"Oh, fuck off."

Take Twenty-Seven

You and Me, Both

How many stars are out there?

Impossible to even quantify. Billions, trillions. Gazillions. Catrillions. Even if they could be counted, we don't have the words.

But I am referring to showbiz stars (celebrities) and not the celestial variety.

Millions of us will take a crack at stardom and in all manner of pursuits: acting, sports, comedy, writing, singing, academia, business, religion… but the odds are firmly against. Most wannabes perish and join the throng of admiring onlookers, gawping at the lucky shiny few.

And I don't mean the fleeting stars like you-tubers or influencers. I mean the properly famous people who are famous forever and even after their death: Elvis, Jackson, Ali, Monroe, Lennon, Einstein…

Few in number, greatly admired and gigantically (over) successful.

People on pedestals and with this, a thought occurred to me during a radio interview with Chris Martin of Coldplay stardom and worldwide acclaim.

Of all the bands founded out of schools and colleges the world over, how many super groups emerge? Not many. A dozen maybe and Coldplay would count on many people's lists.

The interview was to promote their latest album, *Everyday Life*, launched with a quirky approach to publicity. Using only classified ads in local newspapers and two live concerts in Jordan of all places - and live streamed on YouTube.

All very cool, hip and progressive and naturally it gathers acres of conventional media coverage also. The lead story in every arts section of every newspaper but it's real PR coup is being included on the blog of the world renown influencer, Dominic Holland.

And I think this coverage is merited. Coldplay are a great band. They are different. Unabashed, they write anthems, almost modern-day hymns. The song *Yellow* alone, might even be enough. A band loved by millions and so imagine then, being Coldplay's front man. Private jets. Packed stadiums. Gargantuan wealth, acclaim and other accruements besides. We can only imagine.

But then something occurred in the interview which really shook me. Like a slap in my face or a wake-up call which endeared me to this rock star even more.

Let me explain…

The interviewer is gleeful. Thrilled at his exclusive and no doubt on being flown out to Jordan, he put to Chris Martin,

"…you're a big fixture at Glastonbury… you've headlined before and last year, you made an impromptu appearance during Stomzy's set – will we be seeing you again next year?"

An affectionate and flattering question but rebuffed with a harsh and resolute, "no" and an awkward silence followed. The interviewer floundered a little, perhaps wondering if he had missed something. And so he prodded a little further.

Chris Martin went on to explain that he recalled the gig. How he took to the stage unannounced and began dancing and singing along with the grime star – no doubt, to the raptures of the 150,000 watching.

And I thought to myself, how cool to be able to do such a thing. To be Chris Martin.

But then he went on to say,

"It was great fun – but afterwards I saw a tweet…"

You can always rely on him to appear in a tracksuit and ruin things.

He was paraphrasing but this was the gist…

Martin went on to say, "And so I thought, I shouldn't be on-line and I won't be doing that again."

And immediately I thought of ratios again…

Coldplay have over 20 million followers on Twitter.

And no doubt, hundreds of millions elsewhere. Chris Martin is the singer of one of the world's most successful bands. A man living the life and who wants for nothing.

So to hear him laid-so-low by a solitary tweet…

To think of all the people at the festival and the millions more watching on TV nodding with approval, that one tweeter can get through and prick Chris Martin's defences. Someone who I assumed is omnipotent and impregnable – it stopped me in my tracks.

The interviewer too. He asked somewhat incredulously, "Did that affect you then?"

And Chris Martin summed it up perfectly.

'We are all human, right.'

And there we have it. So, thank you Chris Martin.

No matter our success. Our achievements and our place in the world.

Or what we project on to people who seemingly have it all.

Fundamentally we are all the same. Just humans doing our best. We are all fallible and vulnerable in equal measure and fumbling through life.

And understanding this is a good thing. It is a fundamental piece in our defence against the mental health epidemic that we are told is enveloping us all.

Onwards people.

Just do your best and onwards.

Take Twenty-Eight

Good Job, Steve

That feeling when you've lost a complete set of keys!

The hollow sense of dread.

Oh no...

The terror. The creeping paranoia because our keys are access all areas and obviously, they haven't just been mislaid – no, no, someone has them.

And not someone like you and I. You know, decent types with no mal-intent.

No, a miscreant has my keys and is planning to rob me blind. Just waiting for his chance. Probably outside now, sitting in a van with his crew, waiting for my house to be empty - so they can let themselves in and fill their boots.

It is probably normal to catastrophise like this, even though it doesn't really stack up and it certainly does not help. To begin with, during this lockdown, we are never out of the blinking house and so these burglars will need to have the patience of wildlife photographers.

They could take their chances at night but it's a brazen or foolhardy thief because between a Staffordshire Bull Terrier and me up every two hours to pee, they are bound to encounter some resistance.

Another flaw in my thinking, is that my car has not yet been stolen. If they have my keys, why haven't they nicked my car yet?

Logically then, my keys have not been stolen. And this is a good thing.

But then, where are they?

I mean, really.

WHERE THE F**** ARE THEY?

The search goes on and my frustration mounts.

It should be said that Nikki and I are the most energised of the key hunters – with my sons seemingly much less bothered by their loss.

"But Dad, you've got another set of keys, right?"

Every adult knows that there is scant consolation in this logic. Yes, we can still gain access to our dwelling. But the point being, is that so can someone else.

This goes on for days – and soon weeks and still, no keys. But still our car remains - and this gives me hope.

We have searched every possible place they could be – and on multiple occasions, just on-the-off chance.

And all the while, goading me is our dedicated key bowl - a glass bowl within a drawer and specifically designated as a key depository.

This entire drawer and this bowl have been completely emptied on at least three different occasions – just on-the-off chance.

Still, nothing.

I decide that they have been stolen after all. I should really alert the police to be on the look-out for thieves who can't drive.

Defeated, I call a locksmith but they can't come out due to the lockdown and I decide that this is good news. It gives me more time to look. They're bound to turn up, right?

I go online and do a tentative search for a replacement car key and fob and my spirits plummet.

£954

Plus the front door lock will need replacing – and the side gate and quickly I am in to lots of money and my current income as a stand-up comedian is zero.

Come-on-People – we need to find these keys.

I check the key drawer again – you know, just on-the…

My boys remain unmoved, literally. They spend most of their energies coming up with reasons why I needn't panic – in other words why they needn't help.

'But, Dad, we've got nothing to steal.'

This is very true and decent logic.

We have some TV's and an array of mobile phones but little else. Small beer and no interest to professional thieves. There is my computer of course – which contains the manuscript of my latest novel – but if anyone can get this to shift, then I'm all ears. They need only ring the front door bell and I will gladly cut them in.

And so the search continues.

We establish that they aren't under any of the beds or in the shed. Or in any of the bins. Not in the car either.

Then one evening, vanquished, I sit down to watch some TV and facing me is yet another familiar search - for the blinking remote.

The wonder and brilliance of Apple is immediately revoked by the Nazi who designed the Apple TV remote. A device that is specifically designed to fit into even the tiniest crevice.

The mood I am in, I call Patrick down from his room. It's a lair more than a room which I haven't dared enter in lockdown.

Finally, Paddy emerges.

"What?"

This is no way to speak to a parent but I don't have the energy for a row. I need to conserve my energy to be able to shout at the news. Looking at his face, it is apparent that I have interrupted a game he was enjoying with his mates and perversely I am pleased.

'I need you to find the Apple TV remote.'

He senses that this is a grave situation and so without protesting, he makes a start.

He begins by digging his skinny arm down between the tight seat cushions of our newish sofa. An obvious place to look. Too obvious and I am not hopeful.

But then, his face registers something. He's found something but probably just another bloody jigsaw puzzle piece. His cherubic face is excited now as he begins to retrieve his arm. I wait, transfixed. It reminds me of those fishing posts on Instagram.

Finally, his hand breaks free from the cushions and I hear a jangle. I am confused because remote controls don't jangle.

But keys do.

And sure enough, there in Paddy's hand are the missing bunch of keys.

I cannot tell you, the joy.

Once again, our house which contains nothing to steal is safe.

Nikki is elated but confused because she had thoroughly searched that sofa already. Fat fingers I wonder but I don't say this of course, experienced husband that I am.

Well done Paddy and my apologies to the late and great, Steve Jobs. You are a great man after all.

I can now revert to worrying about something else – and with this lockdown I have plenty to choose from.

Take Twenty-Nine

Where do I Apply?

I have wanted to include takes that are not time specific – but this was written in the early stages of lockdown – a time many of us will never forget and so I have included it.

Time used to be that precious commodity but not now, not in lockdown. Time is all that too many of us have. How to fill our days? At least until the day is over and we can waste our evenings with Joey Exotic (the Tiger King) and we wonder why lockdown is playing havoc with our mental health.

Tedium levels are high. The news is full of only one story. Locked at home, I am struggling for focus and have taken to having frequent baths. Time to think and to fret. Because what might I do if the government doesn't allow me to ever do my job again? I ponder career changes and what options I might have. My list of possibilities is not a long one.

Lying in the bath again, I am sufficiently bored to study my shampoo bottle and it does nothing to ease my woes.

The shampoo is Pantene Pro-V Silky & Sleek, a leading brand

in the UK and no doubt across the world, manufactured by the behemoth, Proctor & Gamble.

This particular shampoo is called Silky & Smooth. And I wonder if it is shampoo for people who already have Silky & Smooth hair or for people who wish to achieve Silky & Smooth?

Intrigued, I read on and shortly into the smaller print on the bottle, I have my answer.

"For Frizzy, Dull Hair"

Now, I am no hair expert but I assume that frizzy and dull hair are not desirable characteristics. So if this shampoo is able to transform frizzy and dull (unattractive) in to Silky & Smooth (attractive)…

Then, wow. What a breakthrough this is. And well worth shouting about.

Quickly I turn the bottle around, keen for more information on this miracle product. And unsurprisingly, P&G provide further insights in to their wizardry.

"Gently cleanses while giving hair active Pro V Nutrients…"

I decide that this is very reassuring. To understand that the cleansing is gentle and not aggressive and also to know that I am adding not only 'active' nutrients to my hair but of a Pro V variety. 'Pro V' sounds clinical and technical. I wonder what it stands for. Pro Victory perhaps and presumably in the fight against the frizz.

The bottle goes on to explain…

"Provides silky smoothness & frizz control for hair prone

to frizz or dryness."

Hmm...

Hasn't this already been covered, already? Isn't good writing concise and avoids repetition?

But I guess with a breakthrough as big as quelling frizz and providing 'Silky Smooth' – P&G can be forgiven for going on a bit.

And they certainly do.

On it goes...

For anyone cursed with frizzy and dry hair but might still be doubtful about the efficacy of this shampoo and its capabilities, the bottle then provides the following BULLET POINTS...

• **Fights roughness and controls frizz**

• **Leaves your hair beautifully silky smooth**

• **Leaves hair looking perfectly moisturised**

By now my excitement has evaporated.

Because as a regular user of this premium shampoo, I can't say that my Irish locks have ever felt 'beautifully silky smooth'. I'd say that my hair remains at least quite frizzy and I have no idea whether it is perfectly moisturised. No one has ever told me that it is, anyway.

Not that I would ever do such a thing – but it is tempting just to see the look on the managers face in my local branch of Asda.

Picture the scene…

During this lockdown period, when the food retailers are the unsung heroes of the hour. Having to remain open and exposed and for scant regard. A hard-pressed store manager is called away from his office to deal with an irate customer on the shop floor and with a very unusual complaint.

Tired and frazzled, he stumbles from his office and makes for his store. Ahead of him is a small balding man with dry and frizzy hair. In one hand he clutches a receipt and in the other, he holds a half empty bottle of his best-selling shampoo.

'Yes sir, how can I help?' The manager begins politely because the customer is always right.

'Well…' I begin.

'You can start by answering whether or not you would describe my hair as Silky & Smooth…'

'Er…'

'Or how about perfectly moisturised?'

At this point, I would bow my head so that he can have a good rummage.

But I wouldn't do this of course. It is unfair because I understand that such writing and the spurious claims on a bottle of shampoo is horse-shit. Just filling and not supposed to be read.

So why then does it rankle so much?

Because who gets to write this sort of shit? That's why.

Writers, presumably. Professional writers. Proper writers, the sort who Iron Man can call upon. And if so, how do these writers live with themselves and where the hell do I apply for such a non-job?

Much easier than writing novels and doing stand-up comedy and I venture that it is much better paid as well.

But even more irksome is that I wouldn't have a prayer of securing such a berth at one of these marketing agencies with their achingly naff names like Qnetic or Alfabet.

I imagine these clowns at work in their lofts with pool tables and juke boxes, as they labour over words to fill a shampoo bottle.

"Hey guys, listen up. I think I've got it…"

Jemimah, India, Paris, Piers and Sebastian all hold their breath.

Marcus takes a beat…

How about, "Leaves your hair beautifully silky smooth."

Brilliant. Genius. Instant applause. Some of them burst in to tears.

Nice work if one can get it.

Which like I've said already, I can't.

Take Thirty

Killer Comedy

Given 2020 to date...

...with all my work cancelling, being confined to the house for extended periods and with little to do (no gigs) - plus three of our boys have flown our nest, leaving just three people in-residence plus our beloved and ever popular (and no trouble) dog, Tessa.

You might think that the Holland household would be much more cohesive and efficient as a result. Less people, more space and easier to organise.

But alas, this is not so.

Most people in lockdown have busied themselves with de-cluttering. Finally taking on the classic 'I'll do that tomorrow' jobs. Always a cathartic exercise and worthy on its own even without factoring in the enormous upside of making domestic life so much easier and enjoyable.

Just the wonder of space.

Something we never appreciate until we can see it and can utilise it. Space that can be allocated for specific purposes. Repositories for essential things like: keys, remotes, wallets, pens, scissors, matches, glasses…

But I am afraid that the Holland house remains deeply cluttered. Too many boys and for too long. We have cupboards that remain no-go areas. Altogether too upsetting. Crammed with stuff that has somehow survived previous culls and one day we will organise. Tomorrow, maybe?

Granted, this is a little left field, but Martin Luther King looms large in our house. I didn't study him at school but Nikki certainly did and her project on the historical figure (Grade A, btw) remains a terrific high point in her life. She mentions this dissertation a lot. Annually at least and certainly whenever the great man is in the news which is frequently of late with matters as they are in the US.

Indeed, given Nikki's thesis (did I mention, Grade A?) I am surprised that Nikki has not been asked to appear on radio and TV for her insight in to what Dr King would make of the on-going debate.

This week and for some reason, Nikki wanted to locate her Grade A rated biography for Patrick but could she find it in our over-run house?

I was not much help suggesting that surely The British Library has a copy.

Nikki ignored her rude and idiot husband and began to hunt high and low for her masterpiece. Unkind perhaps but worth mentioning I feel, that Patrick didn't appear as concerned about its whereabouts as his mum. He wasn't even in on the search.

Nikki though remained determined, uprooting lots of interesting finds like my birth certificate, our marriage certificate and old photos - but no Grade A journal on the great man.

As the hunt continued, I took to the bath because I have a blog to write and I need to think. I have a few ideas ruminating but nothing good enough to write yet or indeed, for people to read. Every week I post my blog with a sense of achievement and foreboding because I need to do it all again next week. A bath then is a good idea. A chance to relax and allow my mind to percolate.

But it is not easy to relax, even in a bath when Nikki is hunting and so noisily.

I add some more hot water as a distraction to the cupboard doors crashing open and shut all over the house.

But then an almighty crash rings out and is followed by a volley of ripe expletives and I wonder what could possibly have caused such a noise?

Oh, and has anyone been hurt?

Naturally I am concerned but not so concerned to actually get out of the bath.

So I call out instead – to find out what has happened and whether I can help? No reply. So I call out again but this time, louder. Still nothing. I tut and leave it a moment before I call out again, even louder again and now with some expletives of my own.

Still no response and now I am irate because my bath moment is over and I still have nothing to write about.

I am angry because I know why there is no response to my calls.

It is because both Nikki and Patrick have their ears in. These wretched little Apple ear-phones that they both stick in their lug-holes and which cause nothing but angst. Firstly because they continually argue over chargers but mainly because I can never be f***** heard in my own f****** house.

Despite my bellowing, I am still being ignored and now I'm so furious, I am about to vacate my bath which will play badly for everyone when suddenly Nikki appears at the bathroom door.

Her face is a perfect study in fury.

As well as this, she makes for a bizarre site because in her hands, she is clutching two heavy and sharp Comedy Awards that I won back in the day when I was funny.

Apparently both of these awards had been stuffed in to a no-go zone cupboard high up in our bedroom. And perilously positioned within the cupboard atop a box so they could not be seen by a person standing on a chair and on tip-toes and with arms fumbling aloft.

And with this fumbling, the awards came crashing down, almost killing the fumbler in the process. And by the look on her face, this is my fault, presumably for winning such awards and then hiding them away.

And in this very moment, I see it now. I see what I can write about. I want to smile but I don't of course. Experienced husband that I am, now is not the time to share my good news.

Nikki is upset.

"I could have been killed."

And later (out of the bath) I reflect on this. The terrible irony if this tragedy had occurred. That my comedy which has provided so much but would eventually make me a widow.

I tried to calculate the trade-offs of this and its cost effectiveness?

I don't share this with Nikki either. Too risky and too soon?

Better to leave it a day or so and maybe better if she reads it rather than hears it. And maybe when I am out of our cluttered and over-run house...

Take Thirty-One

The Closing Hole

It's a brave man (or a stupid one) who writes a comic essay about women and sport, so here goes…

A fair warning to you all; this *Take* might not read quite so easily. But it all happens to be true. I do not offer opinions but merely present the facts (mostly).

Some years ago, a golf pro saw me coming and promptly sold me a new Driver. For the uninitiated, the Driver is the golf club that has the longest shaft, the biggest head and hits the golf ball the furthest distance.

Affectionately known as the Big Dog, the Daddy, the Big Gun… it is the club that golfers most enjoy hitting well.

Or male golfers, anyway.

My instincts tell me to pause here for a moment…

Because some readers might need to catch their breath. And perhaps re-read the previous line to make sure that they read it correctly...

Yes, I am afraid you did. But I can explain or at least I will try to.

Those of you still with me. Let's move on.

Of course, it could be that female golfers feel this way too about the Driver but I suspect not all. Being able to hit the golf ball prodigious distances is very useful but because it implies brute strength, muscularity and frankly being butch and manly, I imagine it doesn't preoccupy women in quite the same way.

Anyway, and to the point of this story, this golf pro looked me up and down and suggested that I buy a women's Driver. Quite what this said about me never really occurred to me. I just wanted to play better golf and I didn't care how.

Because men and women's golf clubs are not the same. They are designed to reflect and accommodate the differences in the sizes and strengths between the genders.

The ladies club that I bought had a more flexible shaft and is slightly shorter, it had a larger head with a higher degree of loft and is therefore more forgiving (easier to hit) and its design also gave a nod to the feminine with a large splash of pink.

Time for another pause, I feel. And maybe an even longer one this time.

WTF

"Is he saying that our golf clubs need to be easier to hit and have to be adorned with pink..."

No.

I am not saying that. Just that this club did have a higher loft and was heavily daubed in pink. These are facts and they're relevant to this story which I am beginning to regret recounting in print.

Having a ladies Driver in my bag caused much amusement to my fellow playing partners, who all happen to be men. Lots of unfunny jokes about how I should be allowed to play off the women's tee boxes (further forward) since I am using lady's clubs. I even tried to black out the pink livery using a sharpie pen but it never lasted very long with the pink always reappearing like a pantomime dame from a large cake.

Oh, Hello...

But as things worked out, this new club did not suit me, with my ball too often ballooning to the right. Another pro took a look at the club and the man and his conclusion was flattering but expensive.

Apparently, I was too strong for the golf club and I needed to buy a new driver... and naturally, he had plenty to choose from.

Or he suggested, that I might keep the woman's head (more forgiving) and instead that I have a new shaft fitted. A male shaft which is a little longer and dare-I-say-it, stiffer.

Please bear with me...

I am almost done and the payoff is worth it, I hope.

And this is what happened. A new shaft was fitted to the old head to create a brand-new golf club and it provided years of adequate service for a hapless golfer.

And a few laughs along the way too - on various tee boxes as I explained the origins of my golf club and that it was in fact...

…a woman's head on a man's shaft.

Oh, come on!

That's funny all day long. At least it never failed to get a laugh on a tee box but maybe it's different in print and why I have left this *Take* to last. Which might be a mistake because I am rather hoping that readers finishing Dominic Holland *Takes* on life will feel compelled to write an online review and recommend this book to all their friends.

Or not…

About the author

Dominic Holland is a professional comedian of some regard but in reality, his has been a 'nearly' career. Hampered by highly developed and honed self-doubts, prematurely curtailed by diversity and then finally torpedoed by Covid 19.

It took him a year to realise that the American network marketing company he discovered was a scam. Certainly, not a good business equation. It made him a pittance and cost him much self-esteem.

Undeterred and determined to make his own corn, he then qualified as an Uber driver only to be informed that he could not secure the necessary insurance. "Notable Person" was the reason given. Too famous, then? A cruel irony.

And so for now, writing remains his stony path.

His enthusiastic weekly blog continues at

www.dominicholland.co.uk

He runs a lively community on Patreon with frequent on-line meetings/writing tutorials/QnA's which you are welcome to join at www.patreon.com/dominicholland

He is working hard on his sixth novel, a sequel to his first effort, *Only in America*. For now, it remains untitled and as yet has not been read by his wife, Nikki. She will, however, be called upon in due course.

As ever, Dominic fervently believes that this project, Dominic Holland *Takes* on Life will be his writing/career breakthrough. And with it, he will gain the approval of a fictional billionaire/ super hero and finally become a real writer and not just a blogger.

Lightning Source UK Ltd.
Milton Keynes UK
UKHW011436220223
417460UK00006B/126